A Paines Plough and Theatre Royal Plymouth production in association with University of Plymouth, School of Society and Culture

SORRY, YOU'RE NOT A WINNER

by Samuel Bailey

SORRY, YOU'RE NOT A WINNER

by Samuel Bailey

Cast

GEORGIA	Katja Quist
LIAM	Eddie-Joe Robinson
FLETCH	Kyle Rowe
SHANNON	Alice Stokoe

Production Team

Direction	Jesse Jones
Design	Lucy Sierra
Sound & Composition	Asaf Zohar
Lighting	Rajiv Pattani
Movement	Jennifer Fletcher
Assistant Director	Adam Karim
Accent Coach	Elspeth Morrison
Dramaturg	Sarah Dickenson
Casting	Jacob Sparrow
Production Manager	Hugh Borthwick
Touring Production Manager	Rachel Bowen
Company Stage Manager	Verity Clayton
Deputy Stage Manager	Bethany Pratt
Costume Supervisor	Delia Lancaster

SAMUEL BAILEY (Writer)
Samuel Bailey is a writer born in London and raised in the West Midlands. His play *Shook* won the Papatango Prize in 2019. After a sold-out run at Southwark Playhouse, Papatango created a digital version of the play in collaboration with James Bobin. The film was a NY Times Critic's Pick and won Samuel The Times Breakthrough Award at the South Bank Show Sky Arts Awards in 2021. Previously, Samuel has been part of Old Vic 12, the Orange Tree Writers Collective and a recipient of an MGCFutures bursary.

KATJA QUIST (Georgia)
Theatre includes: *Robin Hood: The Legend of the Forgotten Forest* (Bristol Old Vic); *Triple* (The Space); *Twelfth Night* (Orange Tree); *C-O-N-T-A-C-T* (Aria Ents/WEF Productions); *Her Naked Skin* (Circomedia); *Earthquakes in London* (Bristol Old Vic); *Otis and Eunice* (Raucous Theatre/Britten Theatre/Bristol Old Vic Theatre School). Television includes: *Calling the Shots, Clifford*. Katja is a Peter O'Toole prizewinner.

EDDIE-JOE ROBINSON (Liam)
Theatre includes: *Coriolanus* (Sheffield Crucible); *Jekyll and Hyde* (National Youth Theatre/West End); *Othello* (Frantic Assembly/National Youth Theatre/West End); *Save & Quit* (Edinburgh Fringe Festival). Television includes: *Grantchester, Emmerdale, Small Axe, Casualty, Doctors, The One, Ransom*. Film includes: *400 Bullets, How to Talk to Girls at Parties*.

KYLE ROWE (Fletch)
Theatre includes: *Beast of Blue Yonder* (Southwark Playhouse); *The Giant Killers* (UK tour); *Who Cares,*

Digging Deep (Vault Festival). Television includes: *The Devil's Hour, Mood, Young Dracula, House of Anubis, Girlfriends, Coronation Street, EastEnders, Doctors*. Film includes: *Raven's Hollow, Grimsby, Judy*. Kyle is the co-founder of Just Add Milk (JAM) Theatre Company.

ALICE STOKOE (Shannon)
Theatre includes: *American Idiot –* Broadway World Award for Understudy of the Year (West End/UK tour); *Mamma Mia!* (West End); *Sister Act* (UK tour); *An Evening with Sir Tim Rice and Friends* (Sage Gateshead); *Robin Hood* (Salisbury Playhouse); *Dick Whittington* (Qdos/Theatre Royal Newcastle); *Weather to Fly* (OddManOut/UK tour); *Moving Family* (Northern Nomads/Just The Tonic/Edinburgh Fringe Festival); *Romeo and Juliet* (Complete Works/UK tour); *Beauty and the Beast* (Regal Theatre); *Puss in Boots, Aladdin, When the Boat Comes In, Dick Whittington* (The Customs House). Film includes: *The Duke, Poised*.

JESSE JONES (Direction)
Jesse Jones is a theatre director from Bristol. He is a founding member of award-winning company The Wardrobe Ensemble who are associates of Complicité and Shoreditch Town Hall, and have toured nationally and internationally. Jesse was Resident Director at Royal and Derngate, Northampton having won the Regional Theatre Young Directors Scheme award. He is also an alumni of Old Vic 12, National Theatre's directors programme and Bristol Old Vic's Made in Bristol scheme. In 2011 Jesse founded The Wardrobe Theatre where he was Artistic Director until 2015, before leaving

he helped establish the theatre as the leading fringe theatre in the city. He is now also a trustee of Shoreditch Town Hall.

LUCY SIERRA (Design)
Theatre includes: *Story Seekers* (National Theatre/Unicorn); *Signal Fires* (Potential Difference); *Maggot Moon, Icarus* (Unicorn); *The Winter's Tale, Macbeth, Another World* (National Theatre); *Wilderness, Every Day I Make Greatness Happen, Giving* (Hampstead); *Shift* (London International Mime Festival); *Education, Education, Education* (UK tour); *Hansel & Gretel* (Uchenna Dance/The Place); *Snow White and Rose Red* (RashDash/BAC); *Ramona Tells Jim* (Bush); *Duckie's Summer Tea Party* (Hull City); *Ode to Leeds* (Leeds Playhouse, Young Vic); *Cathy, Benefit, We Are All Misfits* (Cardboard Citizens); *The Grand Journey* (Bombay Sapphire Immersive Experience); *A Kid, This Tuesday, Abyss* (Arcola); *The Tempest* (Royal & Derngate); *Calculating Kindness* (Camden People's Theatre); *If You Don't Let Us Dream, We Won't Let You Sleep* (Royal Court); *The Bear* (Improbable); *Sweeney Todd, David Copperfield* (Octagon Bolton).

ASAF ZOHAR (Sound & Composition)
Theatre includes: *Sessions* (Paines Plough/Soho Theatre); *Wild Country* (Camden People's Theatre); *Romeo and Juliet* (Southwark Playhouse); *The Silence and the Noise* (Papatango); *Peter Pan Reimagined* (Birmingham Repertory Theatre); *Whitewash* (Soho Theatre); *Dennis of Penge* (Albany Deptford/Ovalhouse); *The Goose Who Flew* (Half Moon Theatre); *The Shadowpunk Revolutions* (Edinburgh Fringe Festival). Television includes: *Reggie Yates: Extreme Russia, Race Riots USA, Reggie Yates: Extreme UK, Dispatches: Taliban Child Fighters, Reggie Yates: Extreme South Africa.*

RAJIV PATTANI (Lighting)
Theatre includes: *Dawaat* (Tara Theatre); *Straight White Men, Yellowfin* (Southwark Playhouse); *Statements After an Arrest Under the Immorality Act, OUTSIDE* (Orange Tree Theatre); *Winners* (Theatre on the Downs/The Wardrobe Ensemble); *Final Farewell* (Tara Theatre); *Richard II* (LAMDA); *Santi & Nas, Omelette, Heroine, Tiger Mum, 10* (Vaults Festival); *Hunger* (Arcola); *Dirty Crusty* (The Yard); *Dismantle This Room* (Royal Court); *Wolfie* (Theatre503); *Bullet Hole* (Park Theatre); *Babylon Beyond Borders, Leave Taking, Ramona Tells Jim* (Bush); *Nassim* (Edinburgh Fringe Festival); *Roman Candle* (Theatre503/Manchester 53Two/Ivy Studio Greenside/Edinburgh Fringe Festival).

JENNIFER FLETCHER (Movement)
Jennifer Fletcher co-founded The Mostly Everything People and NOVA, touring small-scale work internationally and takes on multiple creative roles in theatre, opera and film. She is currently developing her own work in Cornwall including *We've Been Here* (a collaboration with Agnieszka Blonska supported by Feast, Creative England and Falmouth University); a new musical with Harry Blake and *The Resurrection* as part of St Just Ordinalia. Theatre includes: *Peter Pan, Secret Seven, Beggars Opera* (Storyhouse); *Semele* (Mid Wales Opera/RWCMD); *Don Giovanni* (Longborough Festival Opera); *Much Ado About Nothing, The Tempest* (Grosvenor Park Open

Air Theatre); *As Long as the Heart Beats* (National Theatre Wales); *Anna Bella Eema* (Arcola Theatre); *Rapunzel* (Cambridge Junction); *Thor & Loki* (Vicky Graham Productions/High Tide); *Outlying Islands* (Atticist Theatre); *Jason & the Argonauts* (Unicorn); *Dido and Aeneas* (Bath International Festival/RCM); *Snow Child* (Unicorn/Sheffield Theatres); *People of the Eye* (Deaf & Hearing Ensemble).

ADAM KARIM (Assistant Director)
Adam is a theatre practitioner working as an actor, tutor and assistant director. Theatre includes: *East is East* (The Jamie Lloyd Company/Trafalgar Studios); *Troilus & Cressida* (Shakespeare's Globe); *Macbeth* (Manchester Royal Exchange); *The Madness of George III* (Nottingham Playhouse); *The Wolves of Willoughby Chase, Pinocchio* (Greenwich Theatre); *Macbeth* (Queen's Theatre Hornchurch); *Child of The Divide* (Tamasha/Polka Theatre); *Ready or Not* (Kali Theatre/Arcola); *Thumbelina* (Stephen Joseph Theatre); *Disgraced* (English Theatre Frankfurt). Screen credits include: *After Love* (BFI/The Beaureau); *The Making of Us* (BBC); *Years and Years* (BBC/HBO); *Three Girls* (BBC); *Carol & Vinnie* (BBC); *Daughter* (cineK/Gizmo Films).

ELSPETH MORRISON (Accent Coach)
Theatre includes: *On the Other Hand, We're Happy, Dexter and Winter's Detective Agency* (Paines Plough); *Amelie* (West End); *My Cousin Rachel* (Theatre Royal Bath); *How the Grinch Stole Christmas* (UK tour); *Little Voice* (Theatre by the Lake); *Ink* (Almeida); *Baskerville* (China tour); *Strangers on a Train* (UK tour); *Crazy for You* (Watermill Theatre); *Skellig* (Nottingham Playhouse); *Wolf of

Wall Street (Sun Street); *Napoli Brooklyn* (Park Theatre); *Hogarth's Success* (Rose Theatre, Kingston); *Sketching* (Wilton's Music Hall); *Contractions* (Deafinitely Theatre); *Trouble in Mind* (Print Room); *My Mother Said* (Sheffield Crucible); *Intemperance* (New Vic). Televison includes: *Horrible Histories, Endeavour, Gangs of London, Life after Life, Flatmates, Vera, Citadel, Prime Suspect 1973, Clique, Coronation Street, EastEnders, Eric, Ernie and Me, The Loudest Voice, Das Boot, Picnic at Hanging Rock*. Film includes: *The Railway Children Return, Legend of Ochi, The Mad Axeman, Watcher in the Woods, The Professor and the Madman, The More you Ignore Me*. Radio includes: *X Files: Cold Cases, My Name is Why, The Testaments*.

SARAH DICKENSON (Dramaturg)
Sarah is a freelance dramaturg and associate dramaturg for LAMDA and Paines Plough. Theatre includes: Associate Dramaturg for Royal Shakespeare Company, Production Dramaturg for The Globe Theatre, Senior Reader at Soho Theatre, Literary Manager for Theatre503, New Writing Associate at The Red Room and founder of the South West New Writing Network. She has worked on performance projects and artist development nationally and internationally for a wide range of organisations and theatre makers including: Nuffield Theatre Southampton, Theatre Centre, National Theatre, Bristol Old Vic, Theatre Bristol, Old Vic New Voices, Liverpool Everyman, Champloo, Theatre Royal Bath, Theatre Royal Plymouth, Tamasha, Apples and Snakes, Almeida, Hall for Cornwall, The Fence and Churchill Theatre.

JACOB SPARROW (Casting)
Theatre includes: *May Queen,
Hungry, Really Big and Really Loud,
Black Love* (Paines Plough);
Oklahoma! (Young Vic); *Black Love*
(Kiln); *Hedwig and the Angry Inch*
(Leeds Playhouse/Home
Manchester); *Anna Karenina*
(Sheffield Crucible); *The Curious
Incident of the Dog in the Night-Time*
(UK tour); *Jitney* (Headlong/Leeds
Playhouse); *Carousel, Our Town*
(Regent's Park); *LOVE, Faith, Hope
and Charity* (European tour);
Perspectives (New Views); *City of
Angels* (West End); *Hadestown,
Pericles, Follie, Amadeus* (National
Theatre); *LOVE* (National Theatre/
international tour/film); *Queer
Season, Rutherford and Son, Faith
Hope and Charity, Mr Gum,
Downstate* (National Theatre).

**RACHEL BOWEN (Touring
Production Manager)**
Theatre includes: *Lost Origin*
(Almeida/Factory 42 – Production
Site Manager for The Production
Family); *Future Cargo* (The Place/
Requardt & Rosenberg – TSM); and
the UK and North American tours of
Barber Shop Chronicles (Fuel/
National Theatre – Re-lighter/
Production LX).

**VERITY CLAYTON (Company Stage
Manager)**
Theatre includes: *The Storm Whale*
(York Theatre Royal/The Marlowe);
The Snail and the Whale (Tall Stories/
West End/Sydney Opera House);
Alice and the Little Prince (Edinburgh
Fringe Festival/Lyric Hammersmith);
The Journey Home (Little Angel/
Beijing); *There's a Rang Tan in my
Bedroom, The Singing Mermaid,
WOW! Said the Owl* (Little Angel);
Under the Rainbow (Polka); *Recycled
Rubbish* (Theatre Rites).

**BETHANY PRATT (Deputy Stage
Manager)**
Theatre includes: *Cinderella* (Theatre
Royal Bury St Edmunds); *Small
Change* (Omnibus Theatre); *Captain
Flinn and the Pirate Dinosaurs* (West
End/UK tour); *Can I Help You?*
(Omnibus Theatre/UK tour); *For King
and Country* (Southwark Playhouse).

Paines Plough

Paines Plough is a touring theatre company dedicated entirely to developing and producing exceptional new writing. The work we create connects with artists and communities across the UK.

'The lifeblood of the UK's theatre ecosystem' *Guardian*

Since 1974 Paines Plough has worked with over 300 outstanding British playwrights including James Graham, Sarah Kane, Dennis Kelly, Mike Bartlett, Sam Steiner, Elinor Cook, Vinay Patel, Zia Ahmed and Kae Tempest.

Our plays are nationally identified and locally heard. We tour to over 40 places a year and are committed to bringing work to communities who might not otherwise have the opportunity to experience much new writing or theatre. We reach over 30,000 people annually from Cornwall to the Orkney Islands, in village halls and in our own pop-up theatre Roundabout; a state of the art, in the round auditorium which travels the length and breadth of the country.

'That noble company Paines Plough, de facto national theatre of new writing' *Daily Telegraph*

Furthering our reach beyond theatre walls our audio app COME TO WHERE I'M FROM hosts 180 original mini plays about home and our digital projects connect with audiences via WhatsApp, phone, email and even by post.

Wherever you are, you can experience a Paines Plough Production.

'I think some theatre just saved my life' @kate_clement on Twitter

Paines Plough

Paines Plough Limited is a company limited by guarantee and a registered charity.
Registered company no: 1165130
Registered charity no: 267523

Paines Plough, 2nd Floor, 10 Leake Street, London SE1 7NN
+ 44 (0) 20 7240 4533

office@painesplough.com
www.painesplough.com

 Follow @PainesPlough on Twitter

 Like Paines Plough at facebook.com/PainesPloughHQ

 Follow @painesplough on Instagram

Donate to Paines Plough at justgiving.com/PainesPlough

 Theatre
Royal
Plymouth

Theatre Royal Plymouth is a registered charity providing art, education and community engagement throughout Plymouth and the wider region. We engage and inspire many communities through performing arts and we aim to touch the lives and interests of people from all backgrounds. We do this by creating and presenting a breadth of shows on a range of scales, with our extensive creative engagement programmes, by embracing the vitality of new talent and supporting emerging and established artists, and by collaborating with a range of partners to provide dynamic cultural leadership for the city of Plymouth.

Recent productions and co-productions include *MUM* by Morgan Lloyd Malcolm (with Francesca Moody Productions and Soho Theatre, in association with Popcorn Group), *NHS The Musical* by Nick Stimson and Jimmy Jewell, *Amsterdam* by Maya Arad Yasur (with Actors Touring Company and Orange Tree Theatre), *I Think We Are Alone* by Sally Abbott (with Frantic Assembly), *The Strange Tale of Charlie Chaplin and Stan Laurel* (with Told By An Idiot), *One Under* by Winsome Pinnock (with Graeae), *The Unreturning* by Anna Jordan (with Frantic Assembly) and *You Stupid Darkness!* by Sam Steiner (with Paines Plough).

Theatre Royal Plymouth specialises in the production of new plays alongside the presentation of a broad range of theatre – including classic and contemporary drama, musicals, opera, ballet and dance. They have three performance spaces – The Lyric, The Drum and The Lab. TRP has a strong track record of presenting and producing international work from companies and artists including Ontroerend Goed, Big In Belgium at the Edinburgh Festival Fringe, Robert Lepage and the late Yukio Ninagawa. In March 2019 TRP unveiled Messenger, the UK's largest lost wax bronze sculpture created by the artist Joseph Hillier.

In 2022 Theatre Royal Plymouth will be producing *This Land*, an epic theatrical event, created and performed by citizens of Plymouth, UK and members of the Native American Wampanoag Tribe from Massachusetts, USA.

 Follow @TRPlymouth on Twitter

 Like Theatre Royal Plymouth at facebook.com/TheatreRoyalPlymouth

 Follow @theatreroyalplymouth on Instagram

Theatre Royal Plymouth, Royal Parade, Plymouth, PL1 2TR+ 44 (0) 1752 267222
info@theatreroyal.com www.theatreroyal.com

 Supported by
**ARTS COUNCIL
ENGLAND**

Theatre Royal Plymouth

EXECUTIVE PRODUCER — Mandy Precious

Production Team on SORRY, YOU'RE NOT A WINNER

HEAD OF PRODUCTION — Hugh Borthwick
COSTUME SUPERVISOR — Delia Lancester
HEAD OF TECHNICAL — Matt Hoyle
DRUM & LAB MANAGER — John Purkis
HEAD OF SOUND — Dan Mitcham
DEPUTY HEAD OF SOUND — Holly Harbottle
PROJECT MANAGER — Jason Steen
LIGHTING TECHNICIAN — Darren Lake

Sets by Theatre Royal Plymouth

Senior Management Team

CHIEF EXECUTIVE — James Mackenzie-Blackman
DIRECTOR OF ENGAGEMENT AND LEARNING — Mandy Precious
OPERATIONS DIRECTOR — Helen Costello
DIRECTOR OF AUDIENCE AND COMMUNICATIONS — Dylan Tozer
HEAD OF PROJECT DEVELOPMENT — Seb Soper
HEAD OF WORKSHOP — Brendan Cusack
HEAD OF MARKETING — Phillipa Revest
MARKETING CAMPAIGN MANAGER — Megan Potterton
MEDIA & COMMUNICATION MANAGER — Savanna Myszka
DIGITAL CONTENT AND MEDIA PRODUCER — Chris Baker
TALENT DEVELOPMENT PRODUCER — Ben Lyon-Ross
HEAD OF STAKEHOLDER ENGAGEMENT — Suzi McGoldrick
HEAD OF CONTRACTING — Laura Edwards
HEAD OF FINANCE RISK AND IT — Lewis Eynon
THEATRE MANAGER — Ross Ayling

Board of Directors

Nick Buckland OBE (Chairman), Bronwen Lacey (Vice Chair), Sarah Fysh, Shona Godefroy, Emma Huxham, Imogen Kinchin, James Pidgeon

SORRY, YOU'RE NOT A WINNER

Samuel Bailey

To my Mum,
for everything

Acknowledgments

Thank you to: Chris Foxon, Stewart Pringle, Alex Dickinson and Ed Durbin for letting me pester them about their University experiences; Sol Gamsu for the useful resources; Kate Byers and Rebecca Latham for insightful thoughts on early drafts; Sarah Dickenson for shrewd notes thereafter; Rebecca Durbin for her generous, big-heartedness; Calum Maclean, Daniel Bradley, Elinor Crawley and Abbey Gillett for their invaluable input; Eddie-Joe Robinson, Kyle Rowe, Alice Stokoe and Katja Quist for so brilliantly bringing the people in my head to life; Katie Posner, Charlotte Bennett and everyone at Paines Plough and Theatre Royal Plymouth for believing in the play; Kate Prentice and everyone at 42 for the constant support; Sarah Liisa Wilkinson, Matt Applewhite and everyone at NHB for their hard work; and Dave, Jade, Dan, Kate, Brad, Gemma, Tom, Charity and Chris for, once again, making their way into every line of the play.

Special thanks to Jesse Jones for always keeping calm in a crisis; Christabel Holmes for making it all happen; and my Dad for his guidance.

S.B.

Characters

LIAM, *late teens to mid-twenties*
FLETCH, *late teens to mid-twenties*
GEORGIA, *twenty-two*
SHANNON, *twenty-six*
PRISON OFFICER

Notes

(,) denotes a withholding of speech, an expression of something without words.

(–) at the end of a sentence indicates the next line cutting in.

(…) indicates a trailing-off of thought.

A silence is longer than a pause, and a pause is longer than a beat.

This text went to press before the end of rehearsals and so may differ slightly from the play as performed.

ONE

The car park outside 'Bowl X' – bowling alley, arcade, pool hall – Worcester. Evening.

LIAM, *eighteen, jeans and a hoodie. A football at his feet.*

FLETCH, *also eighteen, tracksuit, holds a can of lager and a small bottle of vodka.*

FLETCH. And I said to him, Jamie, mate, I'm gonna give yer a choice, cus that's only fair, I'm gonna give yer a choice and that choice is either say sorry to me now for what you said or I'll spark you right out front of yer mate and don't think that I won't neither.

> FLETCH *holds out the drinks.*

Vodka or Kroner?

LIAM. I'll wait 'til we get there.

FLETCH. Don't be stupid, no one will be there for another hour. No one *decent*. Have a drink. Do you want the vodka or the can of Kronenbourg?

LIAM. Give us the can, then.

> FLETCH *hands* LIAM *the can.*

FLETCH. It's been rolling around down there for about a week, mind.

> FLETCH *unscrews the vodka bottle and takes a swig.*

Rank.

Shit. Cheers! Here's to you being a clever cunt.

LIAM. Nice one.

> *They bump can/bottle.*

So, what did he say, then?

FLETCH. What did who say?

LIAM. Jamie, obviously.

FLETCH. Right, yeah. He said, 'that's not much of a choice'.

LIAM. Did he? Said that?

FLETCH. He fucking did, you know. So, I said, Jamie *mate*, sometimes in life the choices we get to make aren't always the ones you'd choose, if you follow me, and to be honest the choice between getting your head caved in and saying sorry seems a pretty clear fucking decision, as I see it.

LIAM. Jamie Connolly always was stubborn.

FLETCH. Thick, I call it.

Shall we get some sniff in for tonight? We are celebrating.

LIAM. Yeah, finally getting away from you.

FLETCH. Funny.

LIAM. But I en't getting it from Gaz. Not after last time.

FLETCH. How dare you. He'd have to pay me to take that gak. I get the finest beak in all the shire.

LIAM. Got a number?

FLETCH. Bex'll get us one.

LIAM. Picking her up, are we?

FLETCH. She's on tills 'til eight. After.

LIAM *opens the can, which fizzes in his face.*

LIAM. Shit!

FLETCH. Told yer. Shannon's going and all, you know.

LIAM. What, tonight?

FLETCH. Apparently. Could give her one before you go.

LIAM. *Give* her one before I… She en't interested.

FLETCH. You never think any birds are interested in yer.

LIAM. And somehow you always think they are.

FLETCH. I'm a handsome lad.

LIAM. Yeah, right.

FLETCH. And I've got a big cock. It just gives yer confidence having a weapon like that between yer legs.

LIAM. You do know I've seen it, don't yer? It's like an acorn.

FLETCH. When have you seen it?

LIAM. Loads of times. Every Sunday morning when we played for Colts.

FLETCH. That was under-thirteens! I've had a growth spurt since then.

LIAM. Must have been some spurt. Go on, then. Let's see.

　　LIAM tries to bag FLETCH. FLETCH *fends him off.*

FLETCH. As if. Get away, you bender. I'm en't getting my knob out in a car park like some dogger. Anyway, it'd take too long to get it back in me trackies.

LIAM. Sure it would.

　　LIAM sets down his can and picks up a few small stones. Weighing them in his hand.

　　FLETCH *watches, swigs his vodka.*

　　Be loads of fit girls down there, anyway.

FLETCH. Fit as Shannon Bishop?

LIAM. Yeah, must be. Got to be at least a few in the whole year. Find out tomorrow, I guess.

FLETCH. Posh birds are well frigid.

LIAM. How would you know? You don't even know any.

　　LIAM starts throwing the stones off into the distance.

　　Not aiming for anything. Just throwing.

FLETCH. You'll come back up though, won't yer?

LIAM. Course, yeah. All the time.

FLETCH. For the odd City game and that?

LIAM. Obviously. And I've gotta see my mum, en't I?

FLETCH. I'll pop round. Keep her company.

   LIAM *half-heartedly chucks a stone at* FLETCH.

LIAM. Dickhead.

FLETCH. Nah, she'll miss yer, mate.

LIAM. I'll be back. Loads.

FLETCH. 'Member Pricey's birthday, here? Did that all-nighter after up the rec?

LIAM. Ginge put Macca through *Time Crisis 4*? Yeah.

FLETCH. They still en't fixed it. Fucking Kelly Burton. Spreading shit as usual.

LIAM. Took me weeks to get the top score on that.

   How long's he got left now?

FLETCH. Macca? Eighteen months. Something like that.

LIAM. You ever been to see him?

FLETCH. Once I did, yeah. They've moved him now, down south, some place near London. Got a letter from him. Full of cockney pricks, he said. Could ring 'em and see if they wanna come down the party, if you want? Not Macca obviously… the rest of 'em might be up for it?

LIAM. Could do. It is my last night.

FLETCH. Or just see 'em when yer back next?

LIAM. Yeah… I'll see 'em when I'm back next.

   A beat. They swig.

   FLETCH *pulls out some scratch cards.*

FLETCH. She proper likes yer. Shannon. Always has.

(*Scratching*.) Ah, you little fucker. Nearly had it. They could be cherries, couldn't they?

She's tidy, mate. I'm telling yer. You should have a go.

LIAM. *Have a go*. Do you listen to yourself when you talk? She was in my sets, I think I'd know if she fancied me.

FLETCH. She had that boyfriend, didn't she, then? That fucking nonce Dan Bellamy, getting with her when she was in Year 9 and he was like twenty-fucking-two.

Now, yer leaving, en't yer?

LIAM. And that's a good thing, is it?

FLETCH. Makes you interesting, dunnit? Different.

LIAM. I did actually get with her once. Ages ago, before she was with Ry. That summer we used to hang out on the Biddles' field behind the petrol garage, before they built the new houses on it. We were down there with everyone and you went off with Dave and Matty and Bex had to go in and it ended up just me and her and… Only getting off with each other and that but…

FLETCH. Lucky bastard. You never told me.

LIAM. You were obsessed with her in Year 11.

FLETCH. As if I was. You fucking were. I was riding Jade McEwan in Year 11.

LIAM. After I wrote you that Valentine's card to give to her.

FLETCH. Shit, yeah, that were quality, she thought I was proper romantic. What was it you writ?

LIAM. I almost wish we were butterflies and lived but three summer days. Three such days with you I could fill with more delight than fifty common years could ever contain.

FLETCH. Couldn't get her knickers off quick enough. How you come up with this stuff…

LIAM *laughs, shaking his head.*

LIAM. She going tonight?

FLETCH. Nah, she's got little Mason now, en't she? Never does nothing no more.

(*Scratching*.) These are a joke…

I'd fucking knock Dan Bellamy out if I saw him now. Going out with fourteen-year-olds. Maybe he'll be there later. Do two cunts in one night.

LIAM. Don't know why you bother with them.

Got another can?

FLETCH. Probly. Back seat somewhere.

LIAM *ducks out of view*.

Oi, listen, I was thinking, kid…

LIAM (*off*). Don't hurt yourself.

FLETCH. I was thinking… I could maybe come with yer? Come with yer and… I dunno, get a job or something? I'm sure I could get a job and do that whilst yer at uni and we could get a flat together and it'd be sick, wouldn't it? We could, like… sell weed to all yer uni mates and have parties and that and I'd be dead quiet when yer needed to read all yer books for your course, I've got headphones for my Xbox now…

Cus, like… we've been mates since Year 3 and we could go out and get pissed in town and I thought I'd get a job in a kitchen maybe, like I've always fancied maybe cooking for a job and you've got to start somewhere, haven't yer? We'd pay the rent easy and if you had any problems with anyone I'd be there to help you sort 'em out, wouldn't I?

Lee? What d'yer reckon? Could be a laugh.

LIAM *reappears with a can*.

LIAM. Last one, that alright?

FLETCH. Yeah, sound.

LIAM. Sorry, what was you saying?

FLETCH. I was just… nothing. Just fucking… talking shit. As usual.

LIAM. Win anything?

FLETCH. I reckon her at the Costcutter is selling me duds.

LIAM. They're *all* duds, mate.

FLETCH. I got twenty quid out the fruity at The Poachers the other night.

LIAM. Then what?

FLETCH. What d'yer mean?

LIAM. What did you do with the twenty quid? After you won it.

FLETCH. Well… went back in, didn't it? To get on the megaboard. *But* you need to get on the megaboard to get the jackpot. Fifty quid. See this, here? I could win fifty grand.

LIAM. You've got more chance of getting run over twice in the same day.

FLETCH. Fifty grand.

LIAM. Or hit by lightning.

FLETCH. Fifty grand!

LIAM. Or fucking… I dunno… bumping into Michelle Keegan in Velvet –

FLETCH. Alright, I fucking get it. It's probly not gonna happen. I obviously know that. I'm not thick. I like thinking about it. Thinking about what might happen if I do win. What I might get or whatever. Or where I might go.

Even if I don't win, it gives me a few minutes where it might… happen.

LIAM. When did you go down The Poachers?

FLETCH. Tuesday.

LIAM. You never said.

FLETCH. I text you. You was busy reading yer Shakespeares. I only went with Dave and Matty Sharratt. It was shit. I took the piss out of Matty's eye and he sulked off home.

LIAM. You know he's sensitive about it, mate.

FLETCH. Yeah, well I'd just lost twenty quid, hadn't I? What's he got to cry about?

LIAM. You've got one left.

FLETCH. You've spoiled it now. I'll save it for later. And I won't give you a fucking penny if I win, neither. I'll take Matty and Dave all expenses to the 'Dam and you en't coming.

LIAM *playfully pushes* FLETCH.

LIAM. The 'Dam's shit, anyway.

FLETCH. Now I know you're just being a divvy.

LIAM. Come on. Sorry, alright? Scratch it off.

FLETCH. You've ruined it, I said. Drink yer fucking can.

LIAM. Don't be a bellend.

LIAM *pushes* FLETCH – *who half-smiles.*

What else you gonna spend it on?

FLETCH. Nothing you'd be interested in. None of yer fancy books, yer knobhead.

LIAM *gives* FLETCH *a final push – who shoves back.*

You told yer old man yer going?

LIAM. Nah.

FLETCH. You gonna?

LIAM. Not sure. Might ring him when I'm there. Might not.

FLETCH. Wish our Darren would just fuck off. No offence. Then I'd be able to move back in with me old dear. She said *last* time would be the last time but fucking there he is again, sitting on my settee, watching my telly, eating my dinner.

LIAM. Shagging your mum.

FLETCH. Dickhead.

LIAM. Crash us a fag.

FLETCH. Get fucked, yer already drinking my cans.

LIAM. I'll get some later.

FLETCH. I'll give yer one if you can hit that Astra at the end over there.

LIAM. Which? Blue one?

(*Scrabbling for stones*.) How many?

FLETCH. How many what?

LIAM. How many goes do I get?

FLETCH. Three.

LIAM *weighs the stones in his hand.*

LIAM *hurls the first.*

Nowhere near.

LIAM. Alright, alright. I was getting my eye in.

LIAM *judges the distance more carefully.*

FLETCH. We could go down the driving range tomorrow morning. Hit a few balls. They've got footy golf down there now.

LIAM. Early train. Stop distracting me.

LIAM *throws his second.*

FLETCH. Ooh, close.

LIAM. I reckon I shaved it.

FLETCH. No likey, no lighty.

LIAM *throws the last stone.*

A distant bang. A car alarm blares.

Save yer twos.

LIAM. As if. Cough up.

FLETCH (*pointing towards the car*). Here we go.

WOMAN (*off*). OI.

FLETCH (*shouting*). What?

WOMAN (*off, shouting*). Fucking scallies!

FLETCH gives her the Vs.

FLETCH. Get fucked.

The car alarm stops.

WOMAN (*off, shouting*). Why don't you go and get a fucking job!

FLETCH. Yeah, why don't you fuck off, love! He's going to Oxford fucking University. What have you done with yer life, yer plank! Yeah! Jog on.

(*To* LIAM, *offering a cigarette.*) 'Ere y'are.

LIAM. Sound.

LIAM puts the cigarette behind his ear.

A beat.

FLETCH. Do you have to go tomorrow?

LIAM. What?

FLETCH. Do you have to go? Tomorrow?

LIAM. Yeah, got my ticket booked. I've gotta get settled in and if I leave it later I'll miss all the inductions and everyone will have met everyone else already and I'll be a Billy No-mates, won't I?

FLETCH. Right. But do you wanna go?

LIAM. Do I wanna go? What d'yer mean?

FLETCH. Like… do you really wanna go there?

LIAM. To uni? Yeah, course. Why d'you think I've been going on about it all summer?

FLETCH. Nah, I know. I just mean… You've got in and that, it's fucking quality, mate. Obviously. I don't know no one that's gone to uni. Only you and Matty went to college and he did bricklaying. But do you really wanna go and hang around with all them posh fuckers that go there? Probably all went to the same school together and go… fucking… horse riding.

LIAM. They don't all… do that. They've got footy. And… all sorts. Whatever you want to do.

FLETCH. You know what I mean.

LIAM. Not really. I thought you were sound with it?

FLETCH. You could just stay, couldn't yer? I know lads that'd do anything to shag Shannon Bishop. You both want to. I know you do, you've both fancied each other for years.

We could get a job together, start our own company, I could do the painting and decorating and you could learn to be a sparky…

LIAM. Where's this come from?

FLETCH. I've thought it all through. Pricey's cousin's selling a Sprinter, he'll give it to us well cheap.

LIAM. I don't wanna be an electrician, Fletch.

FLETCH. Well, whatever then. Roofing. I dunno, there's loads of things.

LIAM. It's not that.

FLETCH. You could go uni round here, then. Be just the same, wouldn't it?

LIAM. No, it wouldn't be the same. Not really.

FLETCH. How do you even fucking get to Oxford?

LIAM. On a train. I showed yer.

FLETCH. What's wrong with staying round here?

LIAM. Nothing. I just…

FLETCH. Just what?

LIAM. Because it's Oxford, mate. Oxford University. It's… the best. It's opportunity, and possibility. And all the history. All these mad writers and poets like, Percy Shelley and Oscar Wilde, and I dunno… loads. Nobel Prize winners! All these people that went there and did amazing things.

It's my chance to do something. If I go there and work hard. Get a good degree. Then I'll be… part of that, somehow. I don't know.

It's Oxford, mate. That means something.

A pause.

FLETCH. Who are they, then? Yer new mates? That you met on yer… open day or whatever.

LIAM. What? No, they're not… you must have heard of Oscar –

FLETCH. Always gotta be joeying off, you.

LIAM. Joeying off?

FLETCH. Yeah. Fucking off. Always getting new mates. You did it with Matty in Year 5 –

LIAM. Year 5? Are you actually joking?

FLETCH. No! Matty in Year 5, 'til his eye went manky and he had to take the time off school, then you wanted to be my best mate again. You did it with Dean Butterfield when he got that air rifle and –

LIAM. That was two weeks. You'd gone to see yer nan.

FLETCH. Yeah and by the time I got back you two were proper fucking pally, weren't yer? I'm yer mate. I've been yer mate since we were six. *That* should mean something. That should mean you don't just…

Leave.

LIAM. It does. Course it does. I en't leaving, I'm just gonna be somewhere else for a bit.

Don't you ever wanna do something different?

A silence.

FLETCH. Let's go get Bex.

LIAM. Alright.

> FLETCH *slides off the bonnet of the car.*

Who do you know that wants to get with Shannon, anyway?

FLETCH. What?

LIAM. Shannon.

FLETCH. What about her?

LIAM. You just said. You know loads of people that want to get with her.

FLETCH. Yeah. So what? She's fit, course lads want to get with her. Jealous?

LIAM. No, I just… Like who?

FLETCH. Loads of lads. Jamie Connolly for one.

LIAM. Jay Connolly said that?

FLETCH. Not as polite as I'm putting it.

LIAM. Said that when you saw him?

FLETCH. S'right. What was it he called her? Prick-tease. Wanted to know if you were going tonight and all.

LIAM. Me? Is he coming?

FLETCH. He was. Before I bottled him.

> *A beat.*

LIAM. Before you what?

FLETCH. You heard. And his little bumboy Danny Martin.

LIAM. You're not serious.

FLETCH. I am actually.

LIAM. Fletch.

FLETCH. You should have seen his face. Should have took a picture for yer. He couldn't believe I'd done it. I could see it. Couldn't actually get his head round it. Proper confused.

LIAM. ,

FLETCH. What?

LIAM. For fuck's sake.

FLETCH. I told yer. I gave him a choice.

LIAM. A choice?

FLETCH. Apologise or get a fucking slap.

LIAM. Yeah, a slap. Not fucking… not bottling him, Fletch.

FLETCH. What you getting all mardy for?

LIAM. What am I getting all mardy for? I wonder. What did he do? What happened?

FLETCH. I just said what happened. I bottled him. I've wanted to do it for years, to be honest.

LIAM. Yeah, but why?

FLETCH. Why not? He's a fucking prick. He was a prick at school, he's a prick now.

You were supposed to meet me down there.

LIAM. What? If I'd have come down it might not have happened?

FLETCH. Nah, could have got some digs in. You never liked him, neither.

LIAM. Did anyone see you?

FLETCH. It were a busy pub, kid. I reckon someone *might* have seen me smash two lads with a bottle, yeah. I were gonna leave Danny but he swung for me, the knobhead. It was self-defence, that one.

LIAM. Maybe you do fancy doing summat else? Nice little cell next to Macca?

FLETCH. Oh, give it a rest. I'm going to get Bex. Might get some pills and all.

LIAM. We can't go now.

FLETCH. We fucking can go. We definitely fucking *are* going. It's your last night.

LIAM. Don't do that.

FLETCH. What?

LIAM. Act like everything's normal.

FLETCH. Everything is definitely not normal mate, no, I never said it was normal. You're leaving for one.

LIAM. Therefore, it's alright for you to go around smashing Jamie Connolly over the head with yer bottle of –

FLETCH. Wasn't my fucking bottle, I don't drink Peroni, do I? I had a pint of Thatchers –

LIAM. Whoever's it was! How could you be so fucking thick?

FLETCH. Don't call me thick.

LIAM. What are yer, then?

FLETCH. You should be fucking grateful. I done yer a favour.

LIAM. Doing me a favour would have been using yer fucking head for once.

FLETCH. You know what your problem is? You think yer better than everyone. You think yer better than me.

LIAM. What?

FLETCH. Always have, en't yer?

LIAM. When have I ever said that? Not once have I ever said that.

FLETCH. But you think it, don't yer? Fucking deny it.

FLETCH *pushes* LIAM *lightly to reinforce his words.*

LIAM. Don't push me, Fletch.

FLETCH. Yeah, what you gonna do?

LIAM *pushes back, harder.*

LIAM. Everything has to be about you. How you got left out in Year 9. How you're getting left behind because I'm going to uni. I can't help it if you failed all your GCSEs, can I? That you were too fucking thick to pass one single, piece-of-piss fucking test –

FLETCH *grabs* LIAM.

They tussle – FLETCH *holding* LIAM *in a headlock – but* LIAM *isn't a pushover.*

It's not slick, punches are close quarters, knees and elbows.

Finally, as LIAM *gains the upper hand physically,* FLETCH *lands a solid, effective punch.*

The fight is over. LIAM*'s nose is bleeding. Chests heaving.*

FLETCH. Nearly had me there.

Remember when we played Ghully Park in the cup? For Colts? Semi-final. And they had that big mixed-race lad up front? Giving me all sorts of shit, weren't he? Proper handful. Good game. Could see him getting more 'n' more worked up cus I was giving it back, just as hard and about the sixtieth minute he loses it trying to win the ball back, grabs me, chucks me on the ground. Booted me in the leg.

Just as I'm getting up to nut the cunt I see you sprinting from other end of the pitch, head down, pure fucking Zidane and he gets it from both sides. Both got sent off, remember? Semi-final?

LIAM. I remember Andy getting proper angry with us, saying we lost Colts their first final in five years but we couldn't stop smiling. And that just made him more and more pissed off.

FLETCH. You must have run the length of the pitch to get to where I was. Didn't think about it for a second, just head down and got stuck straight in.

LIAM. Yeah, well.

FLETCH. Jamie was coming down with Danny tonight to kick the shit out of yer. Tried it on with Shannon, in Velvet, the other night. And she turned him down in front of all of his mates. Cus she said she was gonna get with you, before you left. Proper embarrassed him, apparently. Him and Danny were having a few in the pub ready to come down and give you a shoeing. Said he never liked yer, always wanted to do it.

Telling me, he was. Right to my face. Laughing. Thought I wouldn't do nothing.

LIAM. Mate.

FLETCH. Thought he could mug you off in front of me. Well, I fucking showed him.

LIAM. I didn't ask you to do that.

FLETCH. You didn't have to, kid.

LIAM *wipes his nose.*

LIAM. It'll be Christmas before you know it. Round mine, yeah? Do presents in the morning. You know Mum loves having someone else to do the dinner for, then go pub or out or whatever. Like always.

You'll be alright, mate.

FLETCH *holds out his last scratch card.*

,

FLETCH. Going-away present.

LIAM. Could be fifty grand on there.

FLETCH. Doubt it.

LIAM. And I never got you anything.

FLETCH. You can pay for the sniff.

LIAM *takes the scratch card and pockets it.*

Jungle on the car stereo.

TWO

Three years later.

A lawn outside Merton College, Oxford. Night.

The end-of-year ball is in full swing – music thumping and lights flashing inside.

LIAM, *now twenty-one, black tie, enters. Bottled beer and a plate of finger food.*

He's quickly followed by GEORGIA, *twenty-two, formally dressed. Champagne flute.*

GEORGIA. I refuse to go without you.

LIAM (*laughing*). You refuse?

GEORGIA. Absolutely. Refuse.

LIAM. That's very dramatic.

GEORGIA. I'm serious! It's London. It's fun, it's busy. It's where stuff happens. You're in the middle of all this... consequence. Like, everywhere around you, things are happening that mean something. And you're part of that. We'd be part of that.

And you're my best friend. Don't leave me with just Angus and Soph. If you don't come we'll... we'll never see each other. We'll make plans to, but we won't. I'll say I'll come and visit and you'll say you'll come for the weekend but we just won't and then we'll stop texting. And then we'll bump into each other at the reunion in ten years and I'll be doing pioneering work and you'll be sad and regretful. Consumed by thoughts of what could have been. And bald.

LIAM *smiles*.

LIAM. Hold on, why have I lost my hair in this hypothetical future of yours?

GEORGIA. Stress. All the negative energy. That's why you should talk to Bhav and take the room. His cousin will hardly be there anyway, he works, like, insane hours. And you'd be just around the corner from us.

LIAM. I thought Harriet was taking it, anyway.

GEORGIA. She got Fulbright. Brown.

LIAM. No way.

GEORGIA. I know.

LIAM. Wow, fair play. Brown.

LIAM *sits on a step.*

GEORGIA. Three years. I still remember Mum and Dad bringing all my stuff through here. Remember my room in second year? Right in that corner. I'd get up every day and look down and just be, like…

I'll miss this place.

LIAM. Yeah?

GEORGIA. Yeah. I mean, there's stuff I won't miss. 8:15 tutorials. Statistics on a Friday afternoon. Alice *Lim.*

LIAM. Formal hall.

GEORGIA. Definitely formal hall, yeah. Weird. Just let me eat my pasta.

LIAM. Right?

GEORGIA. But I'll miss this *place.* Being here. It's kind of amazing, you have to admit.

LIAM. Yeah, it is.

A silence.

Why did you come here?

GEORGIA. What do you mean?

LIAM. To Oxford. Why did you come *here*?

GEORGIA. Like, as opposed to Bristol or Durham or whatever?

LIAM (*wry*). Sure.

GEORGIA. It's a vague question! I'm trying to… work out what you mean.

GEORGIA *sits next to* LIAM.

Well… I think I always wanted to come here. I don't remember a time when it wasn't… sort of the goal? Or part of it. I was clever and I knew that and people told me I should apply, my teachers and my parents wanted me to. So, I did. And there were other people doing it, Thea and Ruby and a guy called Ben Keel, god I'd forgotten about him. He went for Emmanuel at Cambridge but didn't get in, he's at Exeter now. He actually said something really horrible to me after I got accepted and he didn't. Dick. And obviously, Tom was doing Medicine at Edinburgh so I had to make sure I beat him. It just felt… like something I wanted to do. And the balls are fun.

LIAM. Knew it. Only here for the fancy parties.

GEORGIA. Anything for a pretty dress. Nothing to do with the teaching or the lab facilities or job prospects or anything like that.

LIAM. Congratulations, by the way.

GEORGIA. For?

LIAM. First, isn't it, Charlie said?

GEORGIA. He shouldn't be telling people that, it's not confirmed.

LIAM. I'm *people*, am I?

GEORGIA. You know what I mean.

LIAM. He's just proud of you. I'm proud of you.

GEORGIA *playfully shoves* LIAM.

GEORGIA. Thanks.

LIAM. Imperial.

GEORGIA. Yep.

LIAM. Woman in STEM.

GEORGIA. Ugh, that fucking brochure.

LIAM *holds out his bottle for* GEORGIA. *She reluctantly clinks.*

LIAM. Honestly, well done. It's brilliant.

GEORGIA *gets a text.*

GEORGIA. They're thinking of going to Fever.

LIAM. Imaginative. Who's they?

GEORGIA. Soph, Angus. I think they picked up Freddie from somewhere.

LIAM. I thought he couldn't get a ticket for tonight? Didn't see him at dinner.

GEORGIA. He turned up at the entrance and offered Liv three times what she paid for hers, so…

LIAM. Course he did. What about Charlie?

GEORGIA. Off with the Old Alleynians.

LIAM. Right.

They make no effort to leave.

GEORGIA. Why did you?

LIAM. Why did I what?

GEORGIA. Come to Oxford?

LIAM. I don't know. Seemed like a good idea at the time.

GEORGIA. ,

LIAM. Okay, well, I had this teacher. Collins. Mr Collins. Kept banging on about it. Bringing it up at parents' evening. So, I started the application and then I guess it felt good to be doing something no one else was doing. Kind of… special. I didn't really know what it was. Obviously, I knew what it

was, but not properly, like, what it involved. He helped me.
Gave me the money for the bus to my interview.

GEORGIA. That was kind of him.

LIAM. Yeah, he was alright, Collins.

GEORGIA. Sounds like he would have wanted you to come to
London.

LIAM. Oh, you think so?

GEORGIA. Definitely. I mean, what else are you going to do?
You can't go home.

LIAM. Can't I?

GEORGIA. Come on. And do what?

LIAM. I don't know. I'm just saying, it's an option. It's easy for
you, you're from London.

GEORGIA. Barely. And it's not like I'm moving back in with
my mum and dad, is it?

LIAM. No, luckily you can pick one of Charlie's dad's houses
to move into.

GEORGIA. Charlie asked you to live with us. First. Before
Sophie. Which I think was pretty decent of him, considering.
You were the one who said no.

LIAM. I know he did.

GEORGIA. I get it. This place. It's… weird. It's a weird place.
It's not easy for… if you're not… But maybe London will be
different? It *will* be different. And you don't have to hang
around with us if you don't want to. I mean, you have to
hang out with me obviously, but we can just do it in secret.
I won't tell anyone.

You're my favourite person in this whole stupid place, alright?
I won't let you not come to London. I need you there.

LIAM. Favourite in the whole place? Big shout.

GEORGIA. Don't push it.

Look, I'm sorry you didn't get the funding.

LIAM. It doesn't matter.

GEORGIA. It does matter. And that's fine. But you can apply next year –

LIAM. I don't even know if –

GEORGIA. *And* you'll get it, I know you will, and in the meantime, you can get a job. I'm sure if you asked Freddie he'd talk to his uncle –

LIAM (*sharp*). I'm not asking Fred for anything.

Sorry. I thought I was gonna get it, you know, I wanted it.

I want to come to London because I earned it. Not because I…

GEORGIA. You have. Earned it.

A pause.

LIAM. What did that guy say to you? At school?

GEORGIA. What guy?

LIAM. Ben… whatever his name was?

GEORGIA. Ben Keel?

LIAM. Yeah. When you got in and he said… What did he say?

GEORGIA. I'll give you three guesses.

LIAM. Right.

GEORGIA. It's fine. It's, like…

LIAM. It's not fine. It's the opposite of… If I'd have been there I'd have fucking…

GEORGIA. What? Punched him?

LIAM. I don't know. Maybe.

GEORGIA. It did occur to me at the time. What upset me most about it was I thought Ben was my friend. He *was* my friend, he came to my birthday, you know, I liked him. But then when it came down to it, he really believed he deserved it more than me. Not because he worked harder or got better marks but because of... who he was. And that was it.

You can't let it stop you. Or they win.

A pause.

I know. Give me the coin.

LIAM. Why? Why do you want the coin?

LIAM *rummages in his pocket. Pulls out a coin.* GEORGIA *grabs it.*

GEORGIA. We let the coin decide. Heads you come to London?

LIAM. The coin?

GEORGIA. Yep. *Heads* you come to London, tails –

LIAM. No way.

GEORGIA. Come on. Why not?

LIAM (*playful*). This is not a decision for the coin.

GEORGIA. I disagree, I think this is absolutely a decision for the coin.

LIAM. The coin is... Do I audition for a play, or –

GEORGIA. And you gave a very serviceable Richard II.

LIAM. Or try out for lacrosse –

GEORGIA. Well, you can't really blame the coin for that.

LIAM. Not what I do with my life, George.

GEORGIA. Why can't it be? Don't be a wuss. Heads you come to London, tails, you can do whatever you want. Go home. Do TEFL and move to Korea. Whatever.

LIAM. Come on, we should go and find Charlie.

GEORGIA. Charlie's off with his friends. Heads?

LIAM. George.

GEORGIA. I'm not going inside until you call it.

LIAM. Give me the coin.

GEORGIA. Absolutely not. Once I flip it –

LIAM. Give it here.

GEORGIA. No.

LIAM moves to take the coin. They're both laughing.

GEORGIA holds it out of reach.

LIAM grabs GEORGIA around the middle, grasping for the coin.

GEORGIA flips it and it lands on the grass.

They're not thinking about the coin any more.

I want you to come to London.

LIAM. Seriously?

GEORGIA. I seriously want you to come.

LIAM. Heads or tails?

GEORGIA. Heads or tails. And you have to do what the coin says.

A beat.

LIAM. Fine.

GEORGIA. And you'll talk to Bhav?

LIAM. If it makes you happy, I'll talk to Bhav.

GEORGIA. That would make me happy.

LIAM. What do you mean, serviceable? You came to see it twice.

GEORGIA. Alright, you were very good. Okay?

A beat.

They lean in. Just as they're about to kiss, they come to their senses and break off.

LIAM. Sorry, I –

GEORGIA. No, that was my –

LIAM. No, it was… I mean, nothing –

GEORGIA. No.

LIAM. So, it's…

GEORGIA. Yeah.

A beat.

LIAM. One more drink here before we go?

GEORGIA. Good idea.

LIAM. I'll… I'll get them. Same again?

GEORGIA. Yeah, sure. Thanks.

LIAM *goes to say something. Thinks better of it. Exits.*

GEORGIA *exhales. A mixture of excitement and guilt.*

She paces. Stops. Thinks.

FLETCH *enters, carrying a rucksack. One of his hands is bleeding.*

GEORGIA *faces the opposite direction, lost in thought.*

He watches her.

GEORGIA *turns and – noticing* FLETCH *– jumps, slightly.*

Oh. God. I didn't realise there was anyone else out here. Are you here for the… are you looking for the Porters' Lodge?

FLETCH. Nah. Don't think so. I am looking for someone. Didn't mean to scare yer, sorry.

GEORGIA. That's alright. Who are you… Your hand's bleeding. Are you okay?

FLETCH. Oh, yeah. Shit.

FLETCH *wipes his hand. Sucks at the cut.*

It's sound. Bit of a long journey getting here.

GEORGIA. Do you want me to get something for it?

FLETCH. Nah, yer alright. Cheers.

FLETCH *takes a seat and rummages in his rucksack.*

Takes out a bottle of water. Pours some over his hand.

GEORGIA. Are you sure I can't…? Something to…?

Did you say you were looking for someone?

FLETCH. That's right. Goes here.

LIAM *enters holding two champagne flutes.*

LIAM. The beers weren't cold so I got one as well –

It takes LIAM *a beat to recognise* FLETCH.

Fletch?

FLETCH. Alright, dickhead?

FLETCH *gets up.*

LIAM. Fletch?

FLETCH. Yeah.

LIAM. When did you…?

FLETCH. Look smart, kid.

LIAM. Yeah, it's… Fucking 'ell. Alright, mate?

FLETCH. Alright?

LIAM *walks up to* FLETCH *and hugs him. They break off quickly.*

LIAM. What you doing here?

FLETCH. Come to see you, en't I?

LIAM. You've come to see me?

FLETCH. That's right.

LIAM. Just… come to see me?

FLETCH. Well, I en't come to do a fucking degree, have I?

GEORGIA. Should I get a porter or…?

LIAM. No. No, it's okay, sorry. This is… this is Fletch. He's a mate, from home. Fletch this is George. Georgia. She's a mate from… well, here.

FLETCH. Alright?

LIAM. What you done to your hand?

FLETCH. I had to climb over the wall over there. They wouldn't let me in, even though I said I knew yer, they weren't having none of it, but I come all this way so weren't just gonna go back… must have nicked me hand on the way over. It's sound.

(*To* GEORGIA.) Nice to meet yer. I'm Liam's best mate.

GEORGIA *takes* FLETCH's *outstretched hand.*

GEORGIA. Hi. (*To* LIAM.) This is your…?

FLETCH. Best mate, yeah. Oldest. Best.

FLETCH *looks at* GEORGIA *in her dress.*

You go here as well, do yer?

GEORGIA. Um, yeah.

FLETCH. Fair play. Bet they've got a few books and that in there. We had a library but it was basically like a cupboard, really. They always had to order stuff in and then it took months to come. So, I never bothered.

(*Looking around.*) Bit mad this place, ennit?

LIAM. How did you get here?

FLETCH. Train. Came straight here.

Can see why you wanted to come here now. Like that fucking school that was a castle that all them magic fuckers go to in them books you used to read. What they called?

GEORGIA. Harry Potter?

FLETCH. Yeah, yeah. He loved 'em. Lent 'em to me, but not really my cup of tea. Like, why doesn't he just magic his eyesight better? Don't make no sense.

GEORGIA *half-laughs*.

GEORGIA. Where have you – ?

LIAM (*to* FLETCH). How did you know where to come, mate?

FLETCH. It's not that hard. Merton College, Oxford. (*To* GEORGIA.) Showed me the letter the day he got it. Before his mum, even. (*To* LIAM.) I asked people at the station. Got a bit lost but found it in the end.

Here, kid… (*Snatches* LIAM*'s drink*.) Give us a slug of this, I'm gasping for a proper drink. Train took ages and I spent all my discharge on the ticket.

(*Gesturing to* LIAM*'s food*.) You gonna eat that? I'm starving.

LIAM. Yeah, course, have it.

FLETCH *scoops up the plate and surveys the food*.

FLETCH. Nice one.

GEORGIA. Was it… Fletch? Is that right?

LIAM. Like Fletcher.

FLETCH. Call me Chris if you like but I probly won't answer you cus not even me mum calls me that no more. When she is talking to us.

GEORGIA. Have you come from home?

FLETCH. Home?

GEORGIA. Yeah. Worcester?

FLETCH (*to* LIAM.) Have you not told her about me? (*To* GEORGIA.) Like… *Fletch*? Has he not said nothing?

GEORGIA. Yeah, no. *Fletch*. Of course, yeah. It's end of term, exam brain, you know. I can barely remember my own name.

FLETCH (*referring to the food*). This is alright, this.

Big party going on, is there?

LIAM. It's our end-of-year ball.

FLETCH. A ball, is it? Alright, Cinderella.

LIAM. It's a tradition. You know, after exams. Get dressed up. Let off a bit of steam.

FLETCH. Right. (*To* GEORGIA.) Only ever seen him dressed up smart like this before, what... twice?

Our school had a prom, like. Didn't it, Lee? End of Year 11. Nothing swanky like this, they stuck a gazebo up in the car park but everyone was booking limos and renting suits and that. I'd been booted out of school already, like, earlier in the year so I weren't going but all me mates were. Matty, Ginge, that's two of our mates from home, Liam, all of 'em going in a limo together. And I was gutted. It was me own fault obviously but I wanted them to feel bad for leaving me behind so I told 'em it'd be shit and they were benders for going. Only melts go to prom.

So, Liam says come round Matty's anyway, we're gonna have some cans before we go and I thought fuck it, why not? Have a few tinnies, maybe I could get one of 'em to sack it off. I got there and Liam had made them all chip in to rent me a suit. Shoes, the lot. They stopped the limo round the corner and me and Liam jumped out, snuck in round the back.

GEORGIA. Did you get in?

FLETCH. Oh, yeah. Was decent, wannit? Got kicked out before the end cus they caught me dancing with Jodie O'Shea. Was showing everybody else up.

FLETCH *does a little dance move*.

GEORGIA. I can see why.

LIAM. I think what *Chris* is forgetting to tell you is we both got kicked out because I had to pull him off... Who was it? Jack Warren, wasn't it?

FLETCH. I couldn't help it if Jodie wanted to dance with me and not him. He started it.

GEORGIA. What was the other time?

FLETCH. Eh?

GEORGIA. You said there were only two times you'd seen Liam dressed up. Like this.   ,

FLETCH. Right, yeah. My old man killed hisself. So, then. Lee came with me to the... you know.

GEORGIA. Oh, god, I'm sorry.

LIAM. How's your mum?

FLETCH finishes eating. Sets the plate down.

FLETCH. Dunno. En't seen her.

LIAM. What do you mean? You haven't even been back?

FLETCH. No, I *en't*. Told yer, I came straight here. You talk different.

LIAM. No, I don't.

FLETCH. You do. (*To* GEORGIA.) He does.

GEORGIA. Well, we're all a bit different around different people, aren't we?

FLETCH. Are yer? Why? Sounds like a hassle. Not me.

LIAM. Why haven't you been home?

FLETCH. In yer letters, you said I could come here and visit yer. So, that's what I did.

Listen, is there somewhere I can... toilet on the train was out of order.

LIAM. Yeah.

GEORGIA. They're just inside, on the right as you go in.

FLETCH. Sound.

FLETCH puts his hand on LIAM's shoulder as he walks past.

Good to see yer, mate.

FLETCH exits.

A beat.

GEORGIA. Right. So, he's...

LIAM. Yeah.

GEORGIA. Are you okay?

LIAM. Yeah, sorry, I had no idea he was coming. Are you?

GEORGIA. Yeah, no I'm fine. Bit... but, yeah. So, he didn't tell you he was...?

LIAM. Nope.

GEORGIA. Bold.

Cute that you write letters to your friends at home. You never told me that.

LIAM. I don't.

GEORGIA. He just said you did?

LIAM. Fletch hasn't been at home.

GEORGIA. Oh, right? So, where's he been?

LIAM. Away.

GEORGIA. Away where?

LIAM. Just... away.

GEORGIA. Like, travelling or something?

LIAM. Sort of.

GEORGIA. What do you mean, sort of? Why are you being weird?

LIAM. I'm not.

GEORGIA. You are, you're being all cryptic.

LIAM. I'm not. I just –

GEORGIA. Liam? Just tell me?

LIAM. He's, ugh... he's been...

GEORGIA. Liam?

LIAM. He's been in prison.

GEORGIA. Prison?

LIAM. Yeah.

GEORGIA. Like, actual…?

LIAM. Actual prison, yeah. Fuck, I hope he hasn't bumped into Soph or, god, Freddie… I should have gone in with him.

GEORGIA. Why?

LIAM. God knows what he'll say. Could you imagine him and Fred, like…?

GEORGIA. No, why was he in prison? What did he do?

LIAM. Fletch?

GEORGIA. Yeah. What did he do to be there?

LIAM. It's complicated. Well, it's not that complicated, actually. He bottled two lads in a pub. Jay Connolly had a broken jaw and had to get, like, twenty-odd stitches. I don't know what happened to Danny, the other one. Bad enough to put him in the hospital.

GEORGIA. Oh, my god. Why?

LIAM. That's the… complicated bit.

GEORGIA. That's slightly terrifying.

LIAM. He's alright. He's not… dangerous. Or weird or anything. He's just different to here. I'm not sure you'd understand.

GEORGIA. I think it's generally agreed upon that violently assaulting people isn't a *good* thing. Wherever you're from. He seemed nice.

LIAM. He is. Well, I don't know about nice but he's… a mate. A good one. He was just doing what he thought was best. It's hard to explain.

GEORGIA. You've never mentioned him.

LIAM. No.

GEORGIA. Why not?

LIAM. I don't know. I mean, would you? What do you say to people here about him? How would you describe him to Freddie? Or Angus? Or Soph, even.

GEORGIA. But why didn't you tell me? It's obviously a... big part of your life.

LIAM. I don't know. I just couldn't.

GEORGIA. But why?

LIAM. I was scared, I guess.

GEORGIA. Of what?

LIAM. That you wouldn't want to be friends with me.

A beat.

GEORGIA. Has this got anything to do with why you don't want to come to London?

LIAM. No. I don't know.

GEORGIA. Liam. You have to think about you and what you need now. Not anyone else. You worked hard to get here, to this point. And you don't need to feel guilty for being here.

It's okay to move forward. Good, even. And to do that sometimes you have to leave other stuff... behind. Right?

A long beat.

LIAM. Right.

GEORGIA. I'll always want to be your friend.

FLETCH *enters holding some drinks.*

LIAM. Even if I've got a violent chav for a mate?

GEORGIA. Even then.

GEORGIA *gives* LIAM *a hug.*

FLETCH. This you two done then, is it?

They break.

LIAM. Found them, then?

FLETCH. Yeah. Got a bit lost but some lad showed me the way. Got you these.

LIAM *and* GEORGIA *take the drinks.*

Done with uni. Three years, ennit? What all that in there is for? Proper party, that.

LIAM. Yeah.

GEORGIA. Last year we had all food stalls out here, literally anything you can think of and a silent disco and then in our first year it was this, like, casino sort of theme, that was cool. Very, sort of, James Bond.

LIAM. Yeah, that was cool.

FLETCH (*to* GEORGIA). What's the plan then? Going home? Getting a job and that?

GEORGIA. Yeah. Feels weird to think we're finished but… we're moving to London, me and my boyfriend and most of our friends, really. The ones who aren't doing extra study and stuff.

FLETCH. London?

GEORGIA. Yeah.

FLETCH. Never really got why people bother to be honest. Same stuff as everywhere else just costs loads more.

GEORGIA. Well, it's not for everyone.

FLETCH. What's that mean?

GEORGIA. Just… it's not for everyone.

FLETCH. Not for people like me, you mean.

LIAM. Fletch…

GEORGIA. No, I didn't mean that at all. I was just saying it's fine for you not to want to be there. Just like it is for me and Liam to want to go.

FLETCH. Lee? Go to London?

GEORGIA. Yeah.

FLETCH (*to* LIAM). And do what?

LIAM. I dunno. I don't even know if I'm going, mate.

GEORGIA. Whatever he wants.

FLETCH. He can do that back home.

LIAM. ,

GEORGIA. Can he? Really?

FLETCH. Yeah. Obviously.

GEORGIA. This isn't my – shall we just…?

FLETCH. Just say what it is you wanna say, love. Go for it.

GEORGIA. I don't know what you mean. This is just getting –

LIAM. Mate, just drink your beer.

FLETCH. Nah, go on.

GEORGIA. Well, I mean, Liam just told me where you've been and I think, yeah, maybe there are better options, frankly.

FLETCH (*to* LIAM). So, you did know where I was, then?

LIAM. Funny, mate. Come on. Let's just… why don't we go inside?

FLETCH. Cus I was starting to think maybe you never. Or you forgot or summat.

LIAM. Course I didn't forget.

GEORGIA (*to* LIAM). I think I'm going to go inside.

FLETCH. Yeah, off you trot, you toffee-nosed bitch.

GEORGIA. Excuse me? I can just get the porters, if you're going to be rude.

FLETCH. Get 'em, then.

LIAM (*to* GEORGIA). No, don't. Just leave it to –

GEORGIA (*to* FLETCH). You've just turned up, out of the blue –

FLETCH. I've come to see my best mate.

GEORGIA. Fine, well, I'm not staying here to be called all sorts of –

LIAM. George!

FLETCH (*to* LIAM). Three years I was in there and after the first one I barely heard from yer. Few letters, that was it. And you never come to see me once. Not once. You said you would and you never did. Not at Stoke Heath or when they moved me up Gartree. None of the rest of 'em came but I never expected 'em to. You were sposed to be my best mate.

LIAM. I know, mate. I've been here. At university.

FLETCH. So what? I had you down on my approved list. And you never came. And you promised you would.

LIAM. I've had exams. And essays and it's intense and next thing you know a term has gone and –

FLETCH. For three fucking years?

LIAM. No.

FLETCH. You knew where I was. What jail I was in. Matty told yer.

GEORGIA*'s phone starts ringing. She doesn't know whether to pick it up.*

LIAM. Yeah, I knew.

FLETCH. One time. You could have come one time. And that would have been enough. I'd have been sound. But yer too busy swanning around here in yer stupid fucking –

LIAM. So, I'm just sposed to drop everything –

FLETCH. Yeah. You fucking are. For me, you are.

GEORGIA (*to* LIAM). Do you want me to get somebody?

FLETCH. Thought you was leaving?

GEORGIA. I'm checking if my friend is alright?

LIAM. What do you want from me, Fletch?

FLETCH. A bit fucking more, mate. A bit more effort. A bit more like what I showed you –

LIAM. I didn't come because I didn't want to! Not because I didn't know where you were or I forgot or I was too busy. Because I didn't want to. Alright?

Silence.

GEORGIA. I'll come and tell you before we go?

LIAM. Yeah. Cheers.

GEORGIA (*to* FLETCH). Nice to meet you.

GEORGIA *exits.*

They stand in awkward silence.

LIAM. Toffee-nosed? En't heard that in a while.

FLETCH. It's what my mum used to call our Keeley after she moved to the new estate but same difference.

LIAM. She's alright, you know.

FLETCH. Just mates?

LIAM. Yeah.

FLETCH. If you say so.

LIAM. You've got a tattoo on your neck, you bellend.

FLETCH. You seen what you're wearing?

LIAM. Yeah. Fair play.

FLETCH. Normal suit not enough, is it?

LIAM. Yeah, I dunno. It's just what they make you wear.

Look, mate, I didn't mean to –

FLETCH. All yer mates in there, are they?

LIAM. Come meet them, if you want?

FLETCH. I en't got one of them suits.

LIAM. Doesn't matter, I'll sneak you in. Wouldn't be the first time.

FLETCH. I'm alright here.

LIAM. Yeah, yeah. Me too.

A long pause.

LIAM *and* FLETCH. What was it like?

They laugh a bit.

LIAM *gestures – 'You first.'*

FLETCH. It was alright, yeah. Not at first, but you get used to it. Figure out how it all works. This place?

LIAM. About the same. Surprised you didn't go back to watch the City game.

FLETCH. Didn't fancy it.

LIAM. You feeling alright?

FLETCH. I came to get yer. So we can go home. I got out and no one come to get me, so I come to get you.

Matty said you en't been home in ages.

LIAM. Did he? When did you speak to him?

FLETCH. You en't the only one who's writ to me.

LIAM. Didn't know Matty could read, let alone write.

FLETCH. Yeah, well he can.

LIAM. Nah, I was… Was just a joke.

You really think I speak differently?

FLETCH. You *are* different.

LIAM. Right.

FLETCH. Which one's the real Lee? The proper one? You here, or you back home?

GEORGIA *enters. Loiters by the door.*

GEORGIA. Liam. We're going to go.

LIAM (*to* FLETCH). Say sorry and come with us.

FLETCH. What have I got to say sorry for?

LIAM. It'll be a good night. You can crash in my room.

FLETCH. You go. Yer last night, ennit. Don't want me making a tit of myself in front of all yer new mates.

LIAM. Don't be stupid. You've already done that.

FLETCH. Funny.

LIAM. Don't go. How you gonna get home?

FLETCH. Dunno. Jump the barrier.

LIAM. Honestly, it was just a shock, that's all. We'll find you a suit, you'll fit right in.

FLETCH. What? Like you do?

FLETCH *makes to go.*

LIAM. Look, if you won't stay, let me… let me give you something so you can get back. Don't want you getting caught and… Here.

LIAM *holds out a couple of notes.* FLETCH *looks at them. Walks off.*

Mate.

FLETCH *exits.*

LIAM *watches him go. Looks back to* GEORGIA.

THREE

Four years later.

The smoking area of The Glovers pub, Worcester. A bench. A patio heater. Afternoon.

LIAM, now twenty-five, a crumpled shirt. Trying to light a cigarette.

SHANNON, twenty-six, Christmas jumper and a small baby bump, stands behind him.

SHANNON. Thought that was you.

> *LIAM stops trying the lighter. Turns.*

LIAM. Shannon?

SHANNON. Hello, stranger.

LIAM. Shannon. Fucking 'ell. Hi.

SHANNON. I said to Tash when we came in, that looks like Liam on the fruit machine. She said it weren't. And I thought, yeah, he's not the sort to be chucking his money away on them.

LIAM. You know, now and again. Just something to do while I... (*Holds up his pint.*) Stop me looking like a total Billy.

SHANNON. You on your own, then?

LIAM. Yeah, just me.

How are you? Fuck. Shannon Bishop. It's been ages.

SHANNON. I'm good. I'm... yeah, really good. What about you?

LIAM. I'm alright, yeah.

SHANNON. Living in London, en't yer?

LIAM. Yeah.

SHANNON. Where?

LIAM. It's called Kennington.

SHANNON. Ooh, Kennington, la-di-da. Sounds posh that. *Kennington*. That, like, where one of the palaces is or summat, ennit?

LIAM (*smiling*). That's Kensington, I think.

SHANNON. Bet you've got a nice house, or whatever.

LIAM. It's a flat. But yeah, it's alright, I guess.

You still up by…?

SHANNON. No, round here now. Mum's moved, as well. Years ago. Patterdale Drive?

LIAM. Shouldn't you be in The Poachers?

SHANNON. Fancied a change.

LIAM. By the community?

SHANNON. Yeah. Across the road, basically. The kids still hang around outside. Nowhere else to for 'em to go, I spose.

I remember walking past there every day on the way to school, me and Bex getting whistled at by you lot. Thinking you were so cool cus you'd nicked a fag off your mum. Walking behind us the whole way staring at our bums. And all those nights freezing our tits off waiting for one of you to dare one of the others to take us round the back.

LIAM. I never whistled at you.

SHANNON. No, you didn't, to be fair. Never went round the back with me, either.

You en't changed.

LIAM. Have I not?

SHANNON. I mean you look the same. Same as I remember you from back in school. Yer hair's longer, though. Looks nice.

LIAM. I've been meaning to get it cut for ages.

SHANNON. I don't usually like it on lads, think it looks scruffy. But it suits yer.

LIAM. Shan, do you want a drink? Can I get you one, I mean?

SHANNON. You want to buy me a drink?

LIAM. Yeah, if you wanted?

SHANNON. Liam Farrow wants to buy me a drink!

LIAM. It's not a big deal. Obviously not if you here with someone, I don't want to put my foot –

SHANNON. I sort of am, yeah. With someone.

SHANNON *looks down at her bump.*

LIAM. Oh, shit! I'm so sorry.

SHANNON. Yeah. Unless that's your thing, I en't one to judge.

LIAM. Definitely not my thing.

SHANNON. I'm just messing with you, babe.

LIAM. Fuck. (*Referencing the bump.*) Sorry.

SHANNON. It can't hear you. I don't think it can, anyway, I haven't really got round to reading any of the books yet.

LIAM. How did I not see that?

SHANNON. Charming.

LIAM. I didn't mean… Congratulations. How are you finding it?

SHANNON. I mean, I'm back and forth to the loo every ten minutes but other than that it's alright so far, yeah. Good.

LIAM. Who's the dad? Any idea?

SHANNON (*laughing*). Cheeky bastard.

SHANNON *playfully whacks* LIAM.

He's inside.

How long you here for? I could do it for you, if you like. Your hair. I'm still at the salon Thursdays and Fridays. We're open before New Year. Take the sides down a bit, maybe.

SHANNON *assesses* LIAM*'s hair.*

LIAM. Probably head back Boxing Day.

SHANNON. Oh, well. If you change yer mind, you know where I am.

FLETCH (*off*). Shan? Shannon?

FLETCH *enters, matching Christmas jumper. Reindeer antlers.*

You'll never guess who's just turned up. Kelly fuckin' –

SHANNON *quickly pulls her hand away from* LIAM.

SHANNON. Babe, look who I found.

FLETCH. Lee?

FLETCH *takes off the antlers.*

LIAM. How's it going?

FLETCH. What you doing here?

LIAM. You know, what most people do in a pub. Having a drink.

FLETCH. En't they got no pubs in London?

LIAM. There's one or two.

SHANNON (*to* FLETCH). Liam was just saying he's back over Christmas.

LIAM. Might stay 'til New Year. I don't know.

FLETCH. Right. At yer mum's for it, is it?

LIAM. Yeah, man. Keeping an eye on her. She said you'd helped her out with a bit of shopping. I meant to text you, say thanks. So, cheers.

FLETCH. She done a lot for me in the past. If she ever needs anything or whatever, I can... I'm about.

(*To* SHANNON.) Come on, babe, they're gonna do the Secret Santa.

LIAM. Didn't think I'd see you drinking in here.

FLETCH. Well, I en't exactly gonna be in The Talbot, am I?

LIAM. Thought they changed owners?

FLETCH. Geoff told the new 'uns. Still got my picture above the bar. Banned for life.

LIAM. Surprised it don't put all the punters off.

FLETCH *pulls* SHANNON *towards him.*

FLETCH. Never had any complaints.

LIAM. You two, then? Together?

FLETCH. That's right.

LIAM. Congratulations on… How long have you been…?

SHANNON (*pulling away from* FLETCH). Maybe I'll get you two a drink?

FLETCH. Got one on the table, bab. (*To* LIAM.) Year and half? Next month?

SHANNON. Don't pretend you don't know.

LIAM. Oh, wow.

FLETCH. Yeah.

LIAM. So, in the summer when I saw you?

FLETCH. Yeah, well, we hadn't seen yer for a while and everyone was there, ennit, so… didn't seem the time.

FLETCH *shrugs dismissively.*

LIAM. No, fair enough.

SHANNON. How's she doing? Your mum?

LIAM. Oh, yeah. Cheers. She's… alright.

SHANNON. She thinks the world of you, you know. She used to come into Tesco, after you'd gone. She'd always come on to my till even if the queue was long so she could tell me what you were doing. What you were studying. What you was gonna do next. Proud of you.

Are yer still studying and that? Or doing that sort of thing?

LIAM. Nah. That didn't really... I had to jack it in. I work for this, like, management consultancy. It's alright, you know, decent money. Mate from uni sorted me out with it.

SHANNON. Oh, right. Well, that's good.

LIAM. She asked after you the other day. Mum. I almost text you but... She always thought you were a good influence.

SHANNON. God, really?

LIAM. Better than Fletch, shall we say.

SHANNON. Why don't I go get those drinks? What you having, Liam?

LIAM. I can get 'em.

SHANNON. What you having?

LIAM. Just a pint of whatever, cheers. Lager. Sorry.

SHANNON. One lager, one Thatchers and one sparkling water for me. I cannot wait to have a proper drink.

SHANNON *exits*.

LIAM *and* FLETCH *both take out cigarettes*. FLETCH *sparks up*.

LIAM. Can I...? Mine's fucked.

FLETCH *passes* LIAM *the lighter*. LIAM *lights his cigarette, hands the lighter back*.

Shannon Bishop, eh?

FLETCH. S'right.

LIAM. How far along is she?

FLETCH. Five months. Due April.

LIAM. Know what you're having?

FLETCH. Shan wants the surprise and I'm happy with either. Where's your missus? Georgia, weren't it? Not with you and yer mum?

LIAM. No, she was. Going to. But, like, got called in by work last minute, so she's still back at the flat. Then she's off to see her family.

FLETCH. Like it down there, do yer?

LIAM. Yeah, it's... you know. Lots going on.

FLETCH. You never come to Matty's birthday.

LIAM. No, I know. I text him. Had to go on this stupid team-building skiing trip thing with work. Good night?

FLETCH. Yeah, it was decent, proper all-nighter camping round Upton. Skiing?

LIAM. Yeah. Was shit. They all knew what they were doing, so they were all off on the slopes and I had to do these beginner lessons with all the little kids. Spent most of the week on my arse.

FLETCH. Right. How come you got time off now, then?

LIAM. It's... Christmas?

FLETCH. ,

LIAM. Can't believe you're having a kid, mate.

FLETCH. What d'yer mean?

LIAM. I dunno. Just can't quite believe it, it's mad.

FLETCH. What, cus it's with Shannon?

LIAM. No.

FLETCH. Can't believe she'd get with me, is it?

LIAM. No. I didn't... didn't mean that. I'm happy for you, mate, of course I am. Happy for you both.

FLETCH. Listen, you'd fucked off to London and fucking
    forgotten about everyone so, unlucky. She wanted to get with
    me and you missed yer chance with her.

LIAM. For a start, I asked you to come to London when I moved.
    I didn't forget about you. I asked you down for the weekend.
    It was you that never got back to me.

FLETCH. What, so you could be embarrassed of me like you
    were with yer uni mates?

LIAM. I wasn't embarrassed of you, mate, I was just –

FLETCH. You fuckin' were. I was there. Don't mug me off.

    A beat.

LIAM. I wasn't any more embarrassed of you than I was of
    them. Some people in that fucking place they're not…
    I don't think they're better than you, if that's what you think.
    They're not.

    I was embarrassed of you seeing that place and thinking
    I was different. That I'd changed because of it. Which I had.
    Which I have.

    A beat.

FLETCH. Why did you stay there, then?

LIAM. What?

FLETCH. Why did you stay if you never liked it? Why didn't
    you just fuck it off?

LIAM. I… Because… I didn't…

    I dunno.

SHANNON (*off*). Yeah, why don't you just keep yer fucking
    nose –

    SHANNON *returns with the drinks.*

    – out of other people's business! More faces than the clock
    on big Tesco that Kelly Burton. Who even invited her?
    (*To* LIAM.) You'll never guess who we saw in here the other
    day. You'll like this. (*Hands* LIAM *a bottle.*) They were

taking forever changing a barrel so I just got you a bottle, alright?

LIAM. Who?

SHANNON (*to* FLETCH). Tell him.

FLETCH. Dunno what yer on about.

SHANNON. Mr Collins 'member?

LIAM. No way. Collins? He must be getting on a bit now.

SHANNON. I mean, not really? He looked the same, sort of. I guess when you're at school you think teachers are way older than they actually are. Came in with his wife. She was pretty, weren't she, babe?

FLETCH. I always thought he was a bender.

SHANNON *clips* FLETCH *round the back of the head.*

SHANNON (*to* LIAM). He remembered Fletch.

LIAM. Hard to forget someone when they lob a chair at your head.

FLETCH. I never threw it *at* him. I threw it, yeah. He just happened to be there in the way. He never even saw me do it and you were there and all! But oh no, must have been Fletch. You never even get suspended, golden boy.

SHANNON. To be fair, Liam was the only one who'd read any of the books we did in his class. What was that one we did in Year 10 with those two men in America... one of 'em's a bit, a bit slow, and he strangles that woman? By accident. What was it called, I quite liked it?

LIAM. *Of Mice and Men*?

SHANNON. Knew more about it than Collins did. That's why you went off to university and we stayed here.

LIAM. You could have gone.

SHANNON. University? God, no, not for me. I'm a home bird. I like going on holiday but at the end of the two weeks I'm gagging to get on the plane. It's where my family are and everyone I know.

(*To* FLETCH.) It's nothing special but we like it here, don't we?

FLETCH. It's not for everyone.

SHANNON. We've even started on the nursery, en't we? Neutral colours cus I don't know if Fletch said but we're waiting 'til the day to find out.

LIAM. Nice, yeah.

SHANNON. And we got all the safety gates from my sister cus her Harrison doesn't need 'em any more.

LIAM. Right?

FLETCH. Have a fair few cousins on your side, won't he?

SHANNON. Or *she*. Yeah. I'm the last one, actually. Even Tash had one before me. You remember Tash?

LIAM. Yeah, yeah.

SHANNON. She's got two. Different dads but they all get on. Jas has got *three*. Two of 'em's at school. Keeps Mum busy, between 'em. Christmas Day is gonna be *mad*.

LIAM. I bet.

SHANNON. We got one of them karaoke machines you hook up to the telly last year, didn't we? You should have seen Mum, trying to do 'Jolene'. Proper thought she was Dolly Parton, didn't she?

LIAM. Yeah?

SHANNON. And then we all have like a Boxing Day thing, don't we? So, if you didn't end up going back to London, you should come round. They'd love to see you, hear about all yer stuff going on.

LIAM. Yeah, maybe? Look, you two should go in.

SHANNON. We'll all go in. Cold, anyway.

LIAM. I might just, um… I don't want to crash your –

SHANNON. Don't be silly. You can't go.

LIAM. My mum will be… I should get back, maybe I'll pop back down later.

SHANNON. You en't even finished yer drink. (*To* FLETCH.) What have you said?

LIAM. Look, it was proper nice to see you. Both of you. I'm dead chuffed for you. Can't wait to meet him. Or her.

LIAM *is trying not to cry. Trying to hide it. Being busy, picking up his cigarettes, lighter, phone.*

SHANNON. Fletch, tell him? Stop being a dickhead and tell yer mate you want him to stay.

(*Noticing* LIAM.) Babe? You alright?

LIAM. Me? Nah, I'm fine.

SHANNON. You sure?

LIAM (*voice catching*). Yep. Fine.

SHANNON. What's wrong?

LIAM. Nothing.

SHANNON. But you're… Did we, did I say something?

LIAM. No, no…

LIAM *stops. Covers his face with his hand.*

I'm sorry.

SHANNON. Oh, *babe.* Come here.

SHANNON *hugs* LIAM.

FLETCH *stock still.*

What's happened?

LIAM (*muffled*). I dunno. Sorry… Nothing.

SHANNON. Something must have happened.

LIAM *pulls away from* SHANNON. *Sits down.*

LIAM. George isn't not here cus she's working. She isn't even back at the flat. She's been at her parents for a bit.

We went to this wedding, few weeks ago. In this big, old place with all of her mates from school. She was a bridesmaid. And I was feeling nervous about it, you know, I don't know 'em that well and never know what to say at these things. So, I had a few drinks and sort of lost count a bit and I got pretty pissed. Worse than that. Embarrassed myself, really embarrassed George. And as we were driving back, I tried to explain, you know, I didn't mean to get like that, I was just feeling… out of place. And I realised I've been feeling like that a lot. Since I went to uni, really. And now when I come back, I feel out of place here and all, so…

They tell you to go to uni cus you'll meet all these new people and experience all these new things and learn all this stuff and it'll all be sound. Like, it'll only add to your life? But what they don't tell you is to do that, to do all that, you have to be… different. You change a bit to fit in, and then a bit more, so you can be more like the people that seem happy there, like they belong there. And then eventually you end up becoming somebody you never meant to, you know? Someone you don't recognise any more. Someone you don't feel right being.

Sometimes I just feel like I shouldn't never have left.

God, sorry. So fucking stupid. Can't believe I… Out the back of The Glovers.

SHANNON. Don't worry, babe. This place has seen a lot worse.

LIAM. We should be celebrating, not… Fuck's sake.

SHANNON. Don't worry. You know you can always come back here. Always. And we might not always totally get whatever it is yer doing but that don't matter.

Does it, Fletch?

A long beat.

SHANNON *giving* FLETCH *daggers.*

FLETCH. You always was a lightweight.

LIAM *laughs*.

LIAM. Yeah.

FLETCH. You want a game of pool?

LIAM. What?

FLETCH. Sort yerself out, then come say hello to everyone. Don't want 'em knowing what a fanny you are.

LIAM. Right, yeah.

FLETCH. Another pint?

LIAM. You buying?

FLETCH. Fuck off, moneybags. I've got a kid on the way.

LIAM. Fair.

SHANNON. You alright?

LIAM. Yeah. Look, I'm sorry. That's never…

SHANNON *waves it away.*

Glad Pricey or no one saw me. Never hear the end of it.

SHANNON. No need to worry about that, babe. He's on tag.

LIAM. Tag?

SHANNON. Yeah. Got caught on a scrambler that had been nicked. Bloody idiot. They pulled him over on the Tolley Road, ran the plates. It was stolen from up Brum.

LIAM. And they put him on tag for that?

SHANNON. Well, he's saying to them, he didn't steal it and they're like, fair enough. Still had to take him down the station. Stolen goods. So, they take his prints and swab him for the records, to put it in the database and their system matches his, like… DNA or whatever it is to some fag butts they found when the warehouses at the back of the business park got broken into ten years ago.

FLETCH. I told him not flick them fag butts on the floor.

LIAM. No way.

SHANNON. So, they got him for that and all. Breaking and
entering into commercial properties. Handling stolen goods.
Only just about kept his job, didn't he? And they give him
the maximum community service. Stace went mad. Kicked
him out for three days. We had him on our settee. Imagine
that, size of him. It's all bowed in the middle now.

LIAM *laughs*.

FLETCH. No one gets away with nothing round here.

GEORGIA *enters*.

GEORGIA. Sorry, I –

SHANNON (*turning to face* GEORGIA). Kel, I swear to God,
you're lucky I'm second trimester cus –

Oh, sorry, babe, thought you was someone else.

LIAM *stands*.

LIAM. George?

GEORGIA. Hi.

LIAM. What you doing here?

GEORGIA. You haven't been picking up your phone. I've been
worried.

LIAM. Right.

GEORGIA. Are you okay? You look a bit…

LIAM. How'd you know I was here?

GEORGIA. I went to your mum's and she said you'd either be
here or a pub called The Talbot? And I tried there, so…

(*Clocking* FLETCH.) Did you know they've got a picture of
you above the bar?

FLETCH. Yep.

GEORGIA (*to* LIAM). I just wanted to make sure you were
okay.

LIAM. I'm okay.

GEORGIA. I can go if it… If you'd rather I wasn't –

LIAM. No, don't. I'm glad you're here.

GEORGIA. Okay.

> (*To* SHANNON.) Sorry, I'm Georgia, by the way. I didn't mean to just barge in like that.

SHANNON. Don't be silly. Georgia, I'm Shannon. This is Fletch.

GEORGIA. Yeah, we've met, actually. (*To* FLETCH.) I don't know if you remember but…

FLETCH. I remember.

GEORGIA. Cool.

> SHANNON *kicks* FLETCH *in the shin.*

> (*To* LIAM.) Do you want to go somewhere to, um…?

LIAM. Sure.

SHANNON. We're actually having a little, sort of, Christmas party inside with a few mates, if you want to stick around?

GEORGIA. Thanks, but… no, I couldn't. I don't want to intrude.

SHANNON. Oh, go on. Be nice. (*To* LIAM.) Liam, you're not going, are yer?

GEORGIA. It's really kind of you but I think – It was quite a long drive and I'm really not dressed for a party at all, so, honestly, thanks but…

> FLETCH *holds out his reindeer antlers.*

FLETCH. Want a drink?

> GEORGIA *looks to* LIAM. *He smiles.*

GEORGIA. Love one.

> *She takes the antlers.*

SHANNON. Wicked.

SHANNON makes to go in. Turns, goes to LIAM.

I was always happy you left. Not happy, like… I mean…
I think you needed to do it. Even if it en't always been the
best, or you've missed home sometimes, if you hadn't I think
you'd have always been wondering.

She gives LIAM *a quick squeeze.*

(*To* FLETCH.) Come on, you. In.

SHANNON *exits.* FLETCH *delays, then follows.*

LIAM. How are you?

GEORGIA. I'm okay. You?

LIAM. I'm alright. Weird afternoon. You in the mum-mobile?

GEORGIA. Yeah.

LIAM. How're your mum and dad?

GEORGIA. Good. Asking after you. Dad's missing his
Pictionary partner.

LIAM. What did you say to them about coming up here?

GEORGIA. I just said I wanted to spend Christmas with you.
And that maybe they could come and do Boxing Day at the
flat? If you're coming back?

LIAM. I want to.

GEORGIA *slowly approaches* LIAM.

They hug. Tight.

GEORGIA. I'm not sure I know how to help you with this any
more.

LIAM. No, I know.

LIAM *takes the antlers and places them on* GEORGIA*'s
head.*

GEORGIA *holds out her hand.* LIAM *takes it.*

GEORGIA *and* LIAM *exit.*

FOUR

One year later.

HMP Stoke Heath.

LIAM, *twenty-six, and* FLETCH, *twenty-six, sit across from each other.*

LIAM *in casual clothes.* FLETCH *in prison-issue tracksuit.*

FLETCH. Found yer way this time, then.

LIAM. Just about.

FLETCH. Bit out the way, this one, ennit.

LIAM. Two trains and a taxi.

FLETCH. Did he go the wrong way? Shannon says they always take her the wrong way.

LIAM. He did, yeah.

FLETCH. You want to get a car, kid. Twenty-six years old you can't drive.

LIAM. What can I say? I'm fucking useless.

FLETCH. Could have told you that.

LIAM. How's the baby?

FLETCH. Gracie? Yeah, alright, mate. Got pictures of her all round me telly. Threw up all over Shan's Villa shirt the other day. Daddy's girl.

Who told you I was here?

LIAM. Darren, of all people.

FLETCH. Darren? Bet he was grinning from ear to ear when he told yer. Where'd you see that useless prick?

LIAM. Talbot. Still with your mum?

FLETCH. Fuck knows. Probly.

LIAM. Gracie Fletcher.

FLETCH. Bishop. Gracie Bishop.

LIAM. Bishop?

FLETCH. Shannon's last name, ennit.

Fletcher... fuck *him*. That name can go with me, that.

LIAM. I've got my mum's last name.

FLETCH. And look how you turned out. She's gonna be clever, like you. Like Shannon. I can tell.

LIAM. Do they let, like, babies in?

FLETCH. Here? Yeah. Got another visit in two weeks. She don't know what's going on. Just happy to see her dad. Best thing in the world.

You should go see 'em.

LIAM. I will. I am. I'll message her, pop round. Not going back for a bit.

FLETCH. Nah?

LIAM. Few bits to sort out.

FLETCH. How's it going?

LIAM. Better. Started running.

FLETCH. Running? From what?

LIAM. Nah, just like, running. Clear my head. Round the streets and that, home from work. Got a new lad in the spare room, he's alright actually. You'd like him, I reckon. He's a Gooner, but you know...

What about you?

FLETCH. I'm sound. Got something to look forward to this time. And they've got me working in the kitchen, so I asked Zo at The Poachers if I could start there when I get out.

Pot-washing and that. But then maybe have a go at the food, as well. Said she'd think about it.

LIAM. You always wanted to work in a kitchen.

A beat.

I've been thinking about what you said to me. About moving away. In the pub. Last year when we... when I saw you.

FLETCH. ,

LIAM. When I told you that I'd not really got on with uni? And you asked me why I stayed? If I didn't like it and I said I dunno.

FLETCH. I remember.

LIAM. Because fuck them. That's why. The people who act like it's theirs. The libraries. The books. The quads, the classrooms. The space. The quiet. The time. All of it.

Why shouldn't we have some of that? Why shouldn't we be there and be ourselves? They don't even give a shit, it's just normal to them. Don't even look twice at it. Most of 'em went to schools that look exactly the same. Our school was a fucking Portakabin with a hole in the roof. Remember Maths? In the winter?

They keep it for themselves and make anyone who isn't like them feel like shit for taking a small piece of it. Like you don't belong there cus you don't know the right things to say or you're not in on the secret fucking code of how to act. Make you wear stupid suits. Sing songs in Latin. Call it *traditions*. But they're just there to scare you. Make you feel different.

That's why I stayed. Because I should be able to be there and be me and if they've got a problem, that's their problem. Not mine. Because *fuck them*.

A beat.

FLETCH. Been practising that, have yer?

LIAM. Little bit.

FLETCH. It's a good 'un.

LIAM. Cheers.

FLETCH. Better make it count then, eh, kid?

A PRISON OFFICER *enters.*

OFFICER. Two minutes, Chris, alright?

FLETCH. Yeah, sound.

She exits.

LIAM. Don't get long, do you?

FLETCH. You were late.

LIAM. I *was* late. Won't be next time.

FLETCH. Couldn't come see me once when I was doing three years, now I'm doing six months you're gonna be a regular, are yer?

LIAM *pulls something out of his pocket and puts it on the table between them.*

FLETCH *snatches at it and holds it under the table.*

What you doing? You'll get me another thirty days. What is it?

LIAM *gestures to have a look.*

A scratchy? Old... Fruity 500. This is banned, this. How'd you even get it in here?

LIAM (*shrugs*). Thought you might want to have a look.

FLETCH. Some old scratch card? What do I want with this?

LIAM. It's the scratch card you gave me before I left. Remember? The night before I left for uni.

FLETCH. What? This is?

LIAM. Yeah.

FLETCH. I give you this?

LIAM. I took it with me. Stuck it on my wall. Realised I didn't have any pictures so it was sort of the only thing I had to remind me of home. Came with me to London and went in a drawer. When George moved out, she nearly chucked it away. Couldn't understand why I wanted to keep it.

FLETCH. As if.

LIAM. Kept meaning to bring it back to show you. Special occasion or summat.

FLETCH. Pretty special, this.

FLETCH *quickly passes it back to* LIAM.

Probly en't even in circulation no more.

LIAM. Hasn't got an expiry on it. I've looked.

FLETCH. Fifty-grand top prize. I got hundred quid out of one, once.

LIAM. You want to do it?

A beat.

FLETCH. It's yours. I give it you.

LIAM. Alright. How about fifty-fifty?

FLETCH. Fifty-fifty?

LIAM. Yeah.

LIAM *looks behind him to check no one is coming.*

Got a coin?

FLETCH. Have I got a coin?

LIAM. Shit, sorry, yeah.

FLETCH. What did you say that uni cost yer again?

LIAM. Probly about as much as it costs to keep you in here.

FLETCH. Probly less.

LIAM. Fifty-fifty?

FLETCH. Alright.

LIAM. What would you do with it?

FLETCH. Got a good feeling, have yer?

LIAM. Maybe.

FLETCH *shrugs*.

Match three fruits to win a cash prize, then scratch off to find how much you've won... yada yada... yeah yeah.

Okay.

LIAM *looks up at* FLETCH.

Sure?

FLETCH. Go on.

LIAM *scratches the card*.

Picks it up again. Looks at it for a long time.

Go on, then. What's it say?

LIAM *goes to speak*.

End.

A Nick Hern Book

Sorry, You're Not a Winner first published in Great Britain as a paperback original in 2022 by Nick Hern Books Limited, The Glasshouse, 49a Goldhawk Road, London W12 8QP, in association with Paines Plough and Theatre Royal Plymouth

Cover photograph: Rebecca Need-Menear; graphic design: Michael Windsor-Ungureanu

Designed and typeset by Nick Hern Books, London
Printed in the UK by Mimeo Ltd, Huntingdon, Cambridgeshire PE29 6XX

A CIP catalogue record for this book is available from the British Library

ISBN 978 1 84842 894 2

Woodland
CARBON
www.woodlandcarbon.co.uk
NICK HERN BOOKS
Printed on Carbon Captured paper

www.nickhernbooks.co.uk

facebook.com/nickhernbooks

twitter.com/nickhernbooks